The Pocahontas Colored School

A Trip to the Memphis Zoo and the Clash With Jim Crow

9/28/08
To John
David McDonald

David McDonald

The Pocahontas Colored School:

A Trip to the Memphis Zoo and the Clash With Jim Crow

The Pocahontas Colored School
This is a true story. Much of the story, including the dialogue, has been reconstructed from people's memories of events and knowledge of how the events unfolded decades ago.

ISBN 978-0-9817738-0-3

Book Design by Kareen Ross www.KareenRoss.com

Hazel House Publishing

Dedication

This story is dedicated to
Eddie Mae Herron McDonald.

Without the incredible courage it took her to tell my father, Charles McDonald, about the bus trip to the Memphis Zoo, the incident would have died, just another lost tale of our segregated past.

Contents

Introduction

In the South during the 1950s, blacks and whites lived in vastly different worlds. There were rarely African Americans in political positions, or employed as law enforcement officers or lawyers. In professions, such as medicine and education, there were few people of color, and none were in administrative, decision-making positions.

The segregation of the races was administered by a set of laws and customs known as "Jim Crow." Those laws mandated segregation and set penalties for violations.

But the legal penalties for those who did not adhere to Jim Crow were not near as frightening as the Ku Klux Klan, a terrorist organization dedicated to keeping blacks "in their place" by any means necessary. There was no due process with the Klan. A person was guilty if the Klan decided he or she was guilty and the punishment was what the Klan determined it should be. Beatings, torture, and hangings were in their terrifying bag of tricks.

In 1959, the civil rights movement was in its infancy and only a small handful of Southern schools had been desegregated. One of the earliest schools to integrate was in Hoxie, a small town only sixteen miles from Pocahontas, Arkansas.

In Pocahontas, blacks made up only two percent of the population but, unlike Hoxie, its schools did not integrate. Churches, restrooms, and water fountains were also segregated. In businesses, blacks could not be waited on until all white customers had been served. White-owned restaurants did not even allow black people to enter the building; they were required to place their order standing outside the back door and wait, out of the sight of white people, until the order was brought to them. Blacks were forced to sit in the balcony of the local theater and were not allowed to enter through the front door of a white person's house. And, whites addressed blacks as "boy" or "girl" while blacks addressed whites as "sir" or "ma'am."

It was in this atmosphere that Miss Eddie Mae Herron, the black teacher of the Pocahontas Colored School crossed paths with Reverend Charles McDonald, the white minister of the First Methodist Church.

The Preacher and the Teacher

Charles McDonald was the first to rise. He dressed, then went straight to the kitchen and started breakfast. The smell of bacon and coffee quickly spread through the house and one by one the four McDonald boys followed their noses to the food. When the table was set and the food ready, Charles said a blessing and the boys ate quickly. They finished, rushed into the den and glued themselves to the Saturday morning cartoons on television.

Charles' wife and the boys' mother, Lois, crawled out of bed, poured a cup of coffee and sat at the kitchen table. Charles joined her. In a few minutes he planned to walk the short distance to the First Methodist Church of Pocahontas, Arkansas, where he was the pastor. There, he would put the finishing touches on his Sunday sermon and take care of the church business he had not completed during the week. On Saturdays like this he usually was back home around noon.

The telephone rang and Charles went into the hall. He answered and spoke briefly to the caller. Walking back into the kitchen, he stood.

Reverend Charles McDonald, wife Lois, and family around 1959.

Reverend McDonald and the boys in Pocahontas in March 1959.

"That was Mrs. Eddie Mae McDonald."

"Is this another one of your Arkansas relatives I have never met?" Lois asked.

"She's not related. She's a Negro woman and she wants to talk to me at her house. She wants to tell me about something that happened to her earlier this week."

"How do you know her?" Lois asked.

"I don't know her. She said we've never met."

There was no need to even discuss the significance of the call. It was 1959. Charles, a white minister, had never received a call from a black woman asking to speak to him at her home. Blacks and whites were strictly segregated. They went to different schools, churches, and lived in different areas of town. Charles and Lois knew this was not an ordinary pastoral visit.

"What are you going to do?" Lois asked.

"I told her I would be there in a few minutes."

"Let me know what happens."

"I will," he said, walking out the door.

* * *

Charles, like all of us, had already had many teachers in his life. Some had been in the classroom, but there had been many more. One was Julius Scott and he had given Charles a lesson while he was still a college student fourteen years earlier.

It wasn't easy for a college student to get from Arkansas to Michigan in 1945. The country was at war and money was in short supply. Charles didn't have a car or the cash needed for a bus ticket. However, there was a Methodist youth conference about to happen with people like him, coming from all over the United States and he really wanted to attend. So he hitchhiked. He made the trip in one day without an incident: safe and sound.

Charles was a college student at Hendrix College, a small Methodist college in Conway, Arkansas. His plan was to finish Hendrix, attend seminary, then follow his calling into the ministry.

He registered for the conference and was told that he had been assigned to a room with another southerner.

"Where's he from?" Charles asked.

"Texas," said the woman manning the desk. "He's in the room. You can meet him."

Hauling his suitcase down the hall and into his room, Charles found himself face-to-face with an African American man. Never before has he faced a situation even remotely similar. In Arkansas and, for that matter, in Texas, not only would the two men have been assigned different rooms, they would have been assigned to different buildings.

"My name is Julius Scott," the man said, extending his hand.

"Charles McDonald."

They shook hands.

Charles' first inclination was to go back to registration and get a new room assignment. He hesitated.

This is a Christian gathering, he thought. I can't refuse to room with someone because of the color of his skin. That's not Christian.

He unpacked his suitcase and Julius Scott became the first black person that he had ever encountered as an equal.

Charles watched Julius throughout the week. He was talented, popular, and well respected. As impressive as Julius was, he was equally, and maybe more impressive for what he was not. Julius was not shiftless, or lazy, or dumb. He fit none of the stereotypes Charles had been taught.

After he returned home, Charles told his mother about the trip. "Mother, I stayed with a colored man."

"A colored man?" A shocked Evangel Galloway McDonald asked her son.

He laughed, "It's alright, nothing bad happened."

He did not tell his mother the thoughts he was having. Maybe his calling into the ministry was also a calling to speak out from the pulpit against the racial injustice of the day. These were unsettling thoughts. In 1945 no one he knew was talking about race. He didn't even have the vocabulary to express what he was feeling. But, two facts he knew were true. First, Julius Scott was a man equal to anyone at the conference. Then there was the second and more troubling truth: Laws that denied Julius an equal place in society were wrong.

* * *

As he drove over to the stranger's house, Charles' experience with Julius went through his mind. Then his thoughts moved a few years forward when three men, two white and one black had also been teachers. The three never spoke to Charles and would probably not even remember the incident, but they had allowed him for a moment in time to see evil.

* * *

The ground was still soaked from the last night's rain as the Rev. Charles P. McDonald, Jr. walked to the Post Office with the morning mail. Charles was thrilled to be in Holly Grove, Arkansas. He was serving a church as a newly ordained Methodist minister, and he was doing exactly what he wanted to do since he was a teenager.

In 1949, the town sidewalks of Holly Grove were wooden and elevated a few inches above ground. Immediately in front of him, two white men walked side by side, while a lone black man approached from the other direction. The ground on each side of the sidewalk was muddy. The rule, known by all, was that the black man would have to step off the sidewalk to let the white people pass.

It would have taken a minimal effort for the two men to move to single file and let the black man pass by. That's all it would have taken for him to stay out of the mud covering the ground on both sides of the walkway. Instead the men continued walking side by side, forcing the black man to step into the mud and wait for them to pass. Charles watched the entire event in mute silence.

The men's indifference was just one more reminder to blacks of their place in society. Incidences similar to this were everyday occurrences, but something about this was particularly disturbing. Maybe it was the total disregard for the black man's dignity that angered Charles, or it could have been his close proximity to the three men. By the time he had returned to the church office from the post office, he was livid. He directed the anger he felt at that moment toward the men who would humiliate another person and walk away seemingly without thought. His anger was directed at his segregated community, which would sanction this and so many other outrages. And the anger was directed at himself, the Rev. Charles P. McDonald, Jr., an ordained Methodist minister, who had once again witnessed something evil and he had remained silent.

As the twenty-two year old minister thought about what he had witnessed, he believed he had to speak out against this and other acts of discrimination. He had no idea how or when he would do so. This wasn't Michigan. There was no one that he could talk to about what he was feeling and segregation was woven into every thread of the fabric of southern society. It was the law of the land and terrible things happened to people who stood against it. Violence or the threat of violence was probably the most common method of retaliation. Being white was some protection, but it did not grant total immunity. He knew of no movement that would support a protest. The few people he knew who opposed segregation were friends from college and seminary, and they were scattered around Arkansas and the country. He could count their numbers on his hands. The system was overwhelming; it was much bigger and more powerful than a few idealistic men in distant towns.

* * *

From these experiences and others, on the day Eddie Mae Herron McDonald called Charles, he already knew that segregation was wrong. A few years earlier, he and twenty-six other pastors had signed a petition opposing Arkansas Governor Faubus' attempts to keep Central High School segregated.[i]

Even before he received the call from Eddie Mae McDonald, Charles was frequently speaking out from the pulpit to his white congregation about race. To his supporters he was known as a man of principles, but to those who opposed him, he was a "nigger lover." Emotions were high. In larger cities of the south, Jim Crow[ii] was slowly and violently crumbling, but that was not so in the small town of Pocahontas. Segregation still reigned.

In the short time it took to drive the few blocks to Mrs. McDonald's house, Charles passed from the comfortable, spacious homes of the white residents to the smaller, inadequately constructed homes of Pocahontas' poorer black citizens. The walls of the homes did a poor job of keeping out the cold weather of winter and the tin roofs baked the houses in the summer. And unlike the wealthier residences, some of the poorer houses did not even have indoor toilets.

Charles drove up to Mrs. McDonald's home on Smithville Street, stopped, and looked around. Unlike his neighborhood, there were no sidewalks or curbs to channel rainwater away from the homes. Mrs. McDonald lived in a small, wood-framed house that sat back about twenty-five feet from the road that ran in front of her home.

He noticed chicken coops and gardens in place of the green lawns that covered the yards in his neighborhood. And he knew the reason why. For the poor, a yard was a resource that needed to be used. They could not afford to waste the land around their homes producing grass.

In the gardens, the spring rains combined with the warming temperatures were having a dramatic effect on the gardens. The plants were exploding with growth and some of the early summer vegetables were almost ready to yield their bounty.

Charles got out of the car and noticed that the slight chill from the night before still hung in the air. He walked to the front door and knocked. Waiting at the door, Charles did not know that he was about to meet one of his most important teachers.

Lifting the Veil of Silence

Mrs. McDonald came to the door. She was in her forties and he judged her to be about 5' 6" tall. She carried herself with a gentle demeanor but there was a look on her face that was not easy to describe. It could have been sadness, or nervousness, or both. It was hard to tell.

"Rev. McDonald, please come in."

"Thank you, Mrs. McDonald."

"Most people call me Miss Eddie Mae," she said.

Miss Eddie Mae Herron in front of the school.

* * *

In the early 1900s, record keeping in rural areas of Arkansas was sadly lacking. This was especially true for blacks. For that reason, little is known about Miss Eddie Mae and her early life.[iii]

Miss Eddie Mae was probably born in 1910 to Rev. Elder E.D. and Mrs. Alice Berry Hill. Her father was a minister at Mt. Zion C.M.E. Church in Fort Smith, Arkansas. She graduated from Philander Smith College, a historically black college in Little Rock. She then attended the University of Arkansas for graduate studies in education.

Miss Eddie Mae would have encountered staggering barriers in receiving her education, especially at the University of Arkansas.

In the 1950s a story was told about a lone black man, attending the all white law school at the University of Arkansas. "He was forced to sit confined by a white picket fence erected around his desk and chair. When he needed to come and go, he sometimes stumbled over that fence. White people around him sometimes stumbled over that fence, too. And still each day when he arrived, there it was, encircling him, keeping him separate but equal." [iv]

Miss Eddie Mae may or may not have been surrounded by a picket fence but there can be no doubt that she was not welcomed with open arms. Some of the obstacles included stares, racial slurs, and the possibility of violence. It took courage to get up every morning and attend classes knowing that she would confront hatred and prejudice coming from every corner of the campus.

After college, Miss Eddie Mae began her teaching career in 1940 at the Biggers Colored School in Biggers, Arkansas. In 1948 the colored school in Biggers closed and the students were transferred to the nearby town of Pocahontas. The Pocahontas school district was not willing to allow the students to attend their all-white schools, so they purchased the St. Mary's A.M.E. Church on Archer Street to serve as the Pocahontas Colored School. Miss Eddie Mae was hired as the only teacher. The building then became the Pocahontas Colored School during the week. On nights and Saturdays, the Archer Street building served as a community center where the black citizens came for dances, banquets, student events, funerals, and community events. On Sunday the building became the St. Mary's A.M.E. Church. No building was a greater influence to the small African American community of Pocahontas than the Pocahontas Colored School.

Graduation banquet at the school around 1958.

The school was used for social dances on the weekend and church services on Sunday.

By the time Eddie Mae Herron McDonald called Charles McDonald, she had been teaching for eleven years. She had married the Rev. Ollie

McDonald but the name Miss Eddie Mae had stuck. She was a highly respected member of the black community. Pat Finley, who later became Pat Finley Johnson, was one of the students at the Pocahontas Colored School. Her family thought so highly of Miss Eddie Mae that when Lurine Finley was pregnant with Pat, Miss Eddie Mae asked and was allowed to name the baby.

She was more than a teacher to the youth. One of the more appreciated tasks she performed was offering literacy classes for the adults. Pat remembers when Miss Eddie Mae taught her mother, Lurine Finley, to read. Mrs. Finley had received only a third grade education, but thanks to Miss Eddie Mae, she was thrilled to be able to read the Bible before her death.

Miss Eddie Mae was a very private person, seldom talking about her background or her life. She seemed happiest and most alive when she was with her students. And with her students, she strove to have each one reach his or her potential. As a teacher, she found the rare balance of being loving, gentle, strict, and fair. The students learned health, home economics, civics, penmanship, and music. They produced plays and Christmas programs which they performed for the enjoyment of their families and the black community.

The town students would ask Miss Eddie Mae if they could stay overnight at her house and she would often allow it. Because she was diabetic she was very careful about her diet and she kept fresh fruit in a bowl on the kitchen table. When the kids were visiting she would allow them to eat fruit from the bowl. Fresh fruit was something the children's family couldn't afford so Miss Eddie Mae seemed like a very wealthy woman.

As an adult, one of Miss Eddie Mae's former students recalls her classroom as, "a place where I learned pretty much everything I know."[v]

Miss Eddie Mae had a couple of expressions that she would repeat again and again. She believed in reading and she would tell her students, "If you can't read, you can't do anything." Every one that left her classroom could read.

She also believed that her students should speak with good grammar and diction. "Always speak your words plainly and distinctively," was another one of the phrases she repeated again and again.

The world of segregation was brutal and blacks were shown in countless ways that whites thought of them as inferior. But Miss Eddie Mae didn't believe her students were second rate. She treated them well. A miraculous thing happened when the students were treated with respect, dignity, and love. In time, they came to believe in themselves and they also learned to treat others with respect, dignity, and love. Miss Eddie Mae's students came out of the Pocahontas Colored School ready to face the world.

Miss Eddie Mae with her students in the early 1950's. The nurse in the background is there to administer vaccinations.

* * *

Charles stepped into Miss Eddie Mae's house. He was given a seat in the living room and offered tea or coffee. As was the custom, they began with some polite small talk, but the opening conversation was somewhat awkward and brief.

"Rev. McDonald, have you ever heard of 'Colored Day' at the Memphis Zoo?" Miss Eddie Mae asked. Memphis, the nearest large city, was a two-hour drive from Pocahontas.

"No Ma'am, I haven't," Charles answered.

Miss Eddie Mae noticed that Charles had used the word "ma'am." In the South, the word "ma'am" was used as a sign of respect. Jim Crow etiquette dictated that whites never address a black person as "ma'am" or "sir."

"I'm the teacher at the Pocahontas Colored School," Miss Eddie Mae began. "I took my students on a field trip to the zoo this week. When we arrived in Memphis, it was lunchtime, so we drove to Overton Park to eat. The children got off the bus and we were getting ready for a picnic lunch when a police car came at us with sirens blaring and lights flashing. Two policemen jumped out of their car shouting all kinds of vulgarities and racial slurs. One of the officers was swinging his club in the air like he wanted to beat us. We didn't know it but we were in a whites-only area. They acted like we were some kind of filthy animals. If anyone had argued or said anything that they didn't like, it's no telling what the police would have done. All we could do was to tell them how sorry we were. We were scared and we got on the bus as fast as we could."

Two years earlier Charles had been sickened by the news reports of the Central High School integration crisis in Little Rock but this was different. This time he wasn't reading the story in a newspaper. He was sitting in a room listening to another human being tell about the horror that had been visited upon her.

Miss Eddie Mae continued. "We drove directly to the zoo but when we got there they told us we had to leave. We were there on the wrong day. There was a sign at the entrance that said Colored Day was on a certain day of the week. One man kept pointing to that sign, calling us names and acting like we were ignorant and couldn't read."

For a moment Charles thought she was going to cry, but Miss Eddie Mae gathered in her emotions and looked directly at him. "My students watched me apologize to those people while they were abusive and called me and my children such terrible names."

This was the first time he had even spoken to a black person about segregation and he was listening to a woman tell a story that he, his wife, and his children would never experience.

"There was nothing I could do," Miss Eddie Mae said. "I teach my students to respect the law and that policemen are there to help. How can I teach them to respect the law when the police threaten and curse us and call us foul, racist names? What do I tell them now?"

The room was silent. Charles knew that people spoke to clergy hoping to hear something that would help them through their problems. All he could say was, "I'm sorry for what happened to you and I'm very sorry for what happened to your students. It was wrong."

"Rev. McDonald, I had to tell someone. Thank you for coming to see me. You are a good man."

The white minister of the First Methodist Church of Pocahontas got up to leave his first ministerial visit to a black person having offered no words of comfort. There was nothing he could say to her that would change the reality. Black people were second-class citizens and both knew that this would not be the last act of discrimination against her or her children.

He walked out the front door. Shaken by what he had heard, Charles decided to go home and tell his wife what he had just experienced. The work at the church could wait.

For just a moment, Charles sat in the car and he took another look around. He started the car, turned around, and headed back home. When he entered his whites-only neighborhood, he noticed again the well-constructed homes and the attractive lawns. He passed the home of his neighbor, Mr. Dreyer. Dreyer was a World War II refugee from Germany and his landscaped yard was full of flowers. The contrast was stark; a yard full of flowers and landscaping were luxuries that the black residences of Pocahontas, only a few blocks away, could not afford.

Charles drove into the carport and went inside. Lois took one look at him. "What's wrong?" she asked.

The everyday reality for blacks in the South was, for that moment, also a reality for Charles. He sat at the kitchen table, and with tears in his eyes, said to Lois, "Have you ever heard of Colored Day at the Memphis Zoo?"

* * *

Maybe Miss Eddie Mae had heard Charles give a sermon on the local radio station, KPOC. Maybe she heard talk about the white men who were meeting in public and discussing integration. Whatever the reason, she believed there was a white minister who didn't think like the others, and she wanted to tell him about her collision with Jim Crow.

Looking back, Mrs. Pat Finley Johnson, who was part of that trip to Memphis with Eddie Mae, thinks it is possible that Miss Eddie Mae was simply tired of being beaten down. She may have thought she had nothing to lose. It may have been like Rosa Parks in Montgomery, Alabama.[vi] Segregation and Jim Crow had worn her down.

Pat (Finley) Johnson on a better day at the Memphis Zoo in 1961.

For Miss Eddie Mae to talk to Rev. McDonald took courage beyond description. If Charles had reacted poorly to her story, the consequences could have been grave. Charles could have told members of the white community of their conversation, and Miss Eddie Mae would probably have faced retaliation for speaking to the white minister. And the consequences could have ranged from her losing her job to physical violence.

* * *

Miss Eddie Mae and Charles became friends for the remaining two years he served in Pocahontas. They talked and visited several times and would even joke about having the same last name and the possibility that they were related.

When Miss Eddie Mae asked Charles to preach at a commencement service for her eighth grade graduates, he was honored. The words he spoke to the students have been lost, but Charles remembers telling them that they were children of God and that they should be proud.

* * *

Charles never forgot Miss Eddie Mae. This was the first time a black person had sat face-to-face with him and related an experience about segregation. Ten years earlier, Charles had witnessed a black man being forced to stand in the mud in Holly Grove and he had sworn that he would someday stand in opposition to Jim Crow. Once again, in Pocahontas, he made the same pledge. But there was a difference. There was an active and growing movement for civil rights and those who opposed segregation had the force of law on their side. The time to stand up and be counted had arrived.

Within a year of his first conversation with Miss Eddie Mae, his alma mater announced that it would continue its whites-only policy and Charles joined with other

Methodist ministers in opposing Hendrix College's practice of segregation. Four years after meeting Miss Eddie Mae, he stood in opposition to a resolution to bar blacks from a church he served. Eight years after meeting Miss Eddie Mae he was to be the only white person to vote to combine the white and black Methodist churches in Arkansas. The motion to integrate carried by one vote, and, except for Charles, every one in the room voted along racial lines. Ten years after their meeting, he worked to integrate the Methodist Children's Home in Little Rock. In these and every other action Charles made on behalf of racial equality, the memory of Mrs. Eddie Mae Herron McDonald and the bus trip to the Memphis Zoo was never far.

Remembering the Past to Heal the Future
August 20, 2007

I am the son of the Rev. Charles P. McDonald, Jr. and since I was old enough to understand, Dad talked about Miss Eddie Mae and how she influenced the course of his life. On rare occasions, I have told the story to friends and coworkers and most listened with mild interest. Earlier this year, I told a colleague about Miss Eddie Mae. To my amazement, he said, "You are not going to believe this, but the Pocahontas Colored School is now a museum and my son volunteers there." The museum is named the Eddie Mae Herron (McDonald) Center after the very woman who talked to my father in 1959, forty-eight years ago.

Sign in front of the historical school commemorates Miss Eddie Mae.

The Pocahontas Colored School August, 2007.

After a series of emails and phone calls I learned that Miss Eddie Mae had been the only teacher at the Pocahontas Colored School. She died a few years after Civil Rights legislation forced the Pocahontas School District to integrate, and she was buried at the Haven of Rest Cemetery in Little Rock.

I also learned that there were some people in Pocahontas who were on the bus and wanted to meet my parents. On a hot August day, I drove my 81-year-old father and 79-year-old mother to Pocahontas. We arrived at the Herron Center to find a small crowd of people. Two of those meeting us had been on the bus to the Memphis Zoo. Others were there because they heard we would be meeting and they wanted to witness the event. Several remembered my parents, and old friendships were renewed.

There were white and black people, and they ranged in age from a 19-year-old black college student to a 100-year-old white woman. We all looked around the museum and enjoyed talking to each other in what was almost a carnival atmosphere. People laughed and enjoyed the company. Then we took our seats around the room. Once seated, each person shared their experiences, their memories of the early 1950s, or their feelings about the events.

My dad, Charles McDonald, told the group about Miss Eddie Mae and how her story and her friendship impacted him. "It encouraged me and strengthened me to be an advocate all of my life for integration: in the church, in the schools, in all of Arkansas. It really had an impact on my life. I always remembered her as a person of real compassion and real concern for the children and what happened that day."

Rev. McDonald at the Herron Center, August, 2007.

Mrs. Helen McCarroll had been a chaperone and was also the mother of two of the children on the bus. She told about how that day was "a bad time, a real bad time." She retold how a group of white people had gathered around them at Overton Park, seemingly waiting for the police to arrive. When they did arrive, the two officers had come out of the car cursing and threatening the group. One man waved his club in the air, sending a frightening message that he was prepared to begin beating any member of the group. Miss Eddie Mae and Mrs. McCarroll frantically loaded the children back onto the bus while Mr. Rex Harper, the white bus driver attempted to calm down the officers. Again and again Mr. Harper told them that the incident was a "misunderstanding." But the officers wouldn't listen. While the police threatened the school group, the crowd stood and watched. Not one white person lifted a finger in protest.

Driving away, the children repeatedly asked the adults, "What did we do? We didn't do nothing."

I asked Mrs. McCarroll how the adults explained what happened to the students on the bus. She said they did not discuss the event at all. If they had allowed the boys and girls to talk about what happened, they could have gotten angry with the oppressors, and their anger could have led to rage, which could have led them to protest segregation. And to protest segregation could be dangerous. Children needed to accept the way things were and move on.

But Mrs. McCarroll did teach her own children about segregation. She taught them to know their place. It was the law, and to remain safe, her children had to accept the reality and conform. Mrs. McCarroll and her late husband told their children that it was all about skin color. Their skin was black, the others were white, and they must stay away from those with white skin.

"I have been scared of Memphis ever since," she said.

* * *

My mother, Lois McDonald, told how Miss Eddie Mae's story influenced the direction of Dad's ministry and how it strengthened their resolve to teach their children to be accepting of people of different races and religions. And she believes her children and grandchildren do have a fundamental respect for all people, regardless of their differences.

* * *

My brother, Ron, was also at the Herron Center. He remembered the time Dad preached at the Pocahontas Colored School commencement service. Ron talked about his reactions to attending his first black service. On the ride home, referring to the custom of "call and response," speaking words of encouragement and agreement to the pastor's sermon, Ron had asked our dad why people talked while he was preaching. Our dad told Ron that was the way the preacher knew the congregation was paying attention.

We all laughed at Ron's story. Playing to the laughter, he said he was glad people didn't speak during the sermon in his father's church. If they did, Dad would have known he wasn't paying attention. It was one of many lighter moments.

Charles, Ron, Lois, and David McDonald after the gathering at the Herron Center in August, 2007.

I said that I believed I was a witness to something special. After hearing the story for so many years, I was now able to sit and listen to people who actually experienced the event. But I didn't say all that I was thinking because I was afraid I would break down. I believed that what we were experiencing was sacred. To have the high honor to sit in the building that had once been called the Pocahontas Colored School and meet and listen to people who were on the bus was a disturbing experience. Without even knowing it, I had been troubled by the evil of that day almost fifty years ago.

* * *

Pat Finley Johnson spoke. "We knew our place. When something like that happens, what could you do? You couldn't speak up for yourself. You didn't have any rights. How could you – what were you going to do? And who were you going to go to? We had to depend on our parents to guide us in the right way."

* * *

Pat also talked about the remarkable journey of the story of their trip to the Memphis Zoo.

It had taken many years for the story to finally make it back to the Pocahontas Colored School. If Miss Eddie Mae had not told the story to my dad, it would have died, unshared and unrecorded, with those who rode the bus. One more lost story of our shared past. [vii]

"I think it is healing when you can talk," Pat said. Without being aware of it, the people on the bus, my parents, and my family had been shackled by locks we never heard click. I believe there was a healing for all the people in the room, and on August 20, 2007, each of us shed some of those chains.

Maybe, just maybe, by remembering where we have been, we can learn and not go back.[viii]

Pat (Finley) Johnson, Chairman for the Herron Center Board of Directors coordinated the August, 2007 gathering at the historical Pocahontas Colored School.

Ms. Helen McCarroll at the Herron Center gathering. Ms. McCarroll was a parent escort during the 1959 field trip. Two of her children were students. "I've been scared of Memphis ever since," she says.

Lois McDonald and Ms. McCarroll in 2007. In 1959 they would not have been able to meet as equals.

Pat Finley Johnson and Frederick Smith share a moment at the Herron Center.

College student Frederick Smith and friend Robyn Wiley participated in the August 2007 gathering. Frederick is a volunteer for the center.

The Jim Crow sign hanging over restrooms in the Herron Center today serves as a reminder of the past and lessons for the future.

End Notes

[i] The first national showdown over school integration had taken place at Central High School in Little Rock, Arkansas in 1957. Central was integrated, but only after a violent and horrific year for nine black students. In an act of unparalleled bravery the "Little Rock Nine" attended school day after day knowing that their school buildings were full of people committed to stopping integration by any means possible.

[ii] Jim Crow was the name given to the laws and customs that governed segregation.

[iii] Most of the information came from the research of Pat Finley Johnson.

[iv] Beals, Melba Pattillo, *Warriors Don't Cry: A Searing Memoir of the Battle to Integrate Little Rock's Central High* (Pocket Books, 1994), 12.

[v] Dr. Jan Ziegler, Booklet Text and Grant Director, *Eddie Mae Herron Center* (brochure), 14.

[vi] On December 1, 1955, Rosa Parks, a black woman in Montgomery, Alabama, refused to give up her seat and move to the back of the bus. She was arrested and her refusal set off demonstrations that many mark as the beginning of the Civil Rights Movement.

[vii] It was a very remarkable journey. In 1959 Miss Eddie Mae told the story to my father, who told it to his children. Forty-eight years later, I took the story to Freddie Smith, a man who lives outside of Hope, Arkansas, a town almost two hundred and fifty

miles from Pocahontas. Freddie told his son, Frederick, who rode with Charles, Lois, Frederick's friend, Robyn Wiley, and me to the Herron Center. We then found ourselves sitting in the old Pocahontas Colored School with people who rode on the bus to the Memphis Zoo. It took forty-eight years for the terrible story to go full circle.

viii The mission of the Eddie Mae Herron (McDonald) Center is to help individuals, communities, and organizations to identify, protect, and preserve the history and to foster widespread appreciation of and respect for the African American culture." I cannot thank Pat Johnson and the Herron Center enough for their willingness to meet with us. Without Pat and The Herron Center this story would have died with all of us. Without Fredrick Smith and his father, Freddie, our meeting would never have taken place. The Herron Center is located at 1708 Archer St., Pocahontas, AR 72455; Phone (870) 892-4433; http://www.herroncenter.org. I strongly recommend a visit.

* * *

The Carroll family has been a great support to the Herron Center. They also helped arrange the meeting on August 20, 2007. If that wasn't enough Ann and Bill Carroll attended our meeting at the Herron Center, then Ann and Pat assisted in the editing of the story. Thank you.

Printed in the United States
204258BV00005B/223-279/P

9 780981 773803